PRACTICAL G

PRACTICAL GRAPHOLOGY
How to Analyse Handwriting

PATRICIA MARNE

KOGAN
PAGE

First published 1990

Kogan Page Limited
120 Pentonville Road
London N1 9JN

British Library Cataloguing in Publication Data

A CIP record for this book is available from the British Library.

ISBN 0-7494-0231-8
ISBN 0-7494-0232-6 Pbk

Typeset by The Castlefield Press Ltd, Wellingborough, Northants in Bembo 11/12 point.
Printed and bound in Great Britain by
Richard Clay, The Chaucer Press, Bungay

Contents

1. Handwriting Analysis in Business

Industry spends a lot of money each year in assessing staff and training them, yet many employers still find that they have the wrong person for the job. Whether it is psychological tests, intelligence tests, or personal interviews that sway the decision to hire, it is often a hit-and-miss affair.

Graphology as an aid to selecting personnel has been used for many years on the Continent – Switzerland, in particular, automatically has a graphological report on all its banking staff. But it is only recently that it has begun to take off in Britain, where it has never been considered quite proper, perhaps because of the British liking for privacy. Nowadays, when an application form states 'in your own handwriting', the chances are that it is going to a reputable graphologist for a report – which should avoid putting a round peg in a square hole.

The advantage of such a report is that it can weed out unsuitable material and discover the weaknesses and strengths of the writer, his mental and physical stability and health, as well as his potential for future development. This is done without the graphologist's being swayed by looks, manner, attitude and personality (or lack of it).

Because handwriting analysis reveals special aptitudes and skills even the applicant may be unaware of, it can bring to light existing potentialities, sometimes of personnel within a firm; conflicts in an organisation can then be sorted out by appointing staff to more suitable positions. Obviously, most handwriting is analysed for qualifications and specific jobs, but the main advantage of graphology is that it is a very reliable and accurate diagnostic tool, very often confirming what the employer already suspects.

Most organisations require different traits for various positions and all handwriting is looked at individually and judged accordingly. The executive needs different abilities from the salesman, the advertising director from the marketing manager, the accountant from the company secretary, and so on.

PRACTICAL GRAPHOLOGY

Handwriting is like fingerprints; no two samples are identical, and a sample of writing can reveal the writer's inner personality rather than the facade he may show the world. Graphology can present a clear picture of temperament, as well as intellectual, social, work and moral qualities. It can show the trouble-makers, those under stress or strain, and the type of person who may be disloyal to a company.

2. Handwriting and Nationality

Many peoples have contributed to the alphabet we use today, including the Phoenicians, Egyptians, Greeks and Romans. The history of writing is a story of constant change, particularly of style and speed. The first treatise on graphology was written as early as 1632 by an Italian physician, Cammille Baldo of Baldi.

In 1896 Dr Klages, a physician, founded the Graphological Society in Germany, where the government recognised the significance of handwriting in revealing character and personality. Klages was followed by many psychologists and graphologists, including Robert Saudek of Prague and the Swiss Max Pulver, who developed the connection between graphology and the psychology of the unconscious and researched the two main traits, extroversion and introversion.

Adler, the social psychologist, Jung, the spiritual psychologist, and Freud, the fundamentalist, have all been aware of and interested in the close relationship between handwriting movement and the complexities of the psychological personality of the writer.

In France, Germany, Holland and many other European countries, handwriting analysis is employed by business managers and executives, educational psychologists, and psychiatrists. The Central Intelligence Agency of the USA has long used graphology, along with other tests, to assess the character and personality traits of its employees.

There are national characteristics in handwriting as there are in everything else, and these have to be taken into consideration and studied by the graphologist before attempting an analysis.

France

French handwriting was heavily influenced before the Second World War by the convents who taught the 'Sacré Coeur' method, which used covering strokes on letters. This type of script is rarely seen now as French handwriting has become more rounded and larger in the middle zones.

Germany

German handwriting has changed considerably from the angular, spiky Gothic script to a far more relaxed style of writing. In older people there is still a lingering of the aggressive, pointed letters, but the younger generation have a much softer style with a cursive formation, usually slightly upright or slanted to the right and with high ascenders.

The USA

The Palmer method of handwriting is popular in the USA and taught in many schools. It is immature to the English eye, free-flowing with a rounded, 'garland' type of formation, especially noticeable in the small *a*s, *o*s, *m*s and *w*s. A feature of the Palmer method is its lack of shading. The up- and down-strokes are of equal pressure. There is also a tendency to add superfluous initial and ending strokes which impede the rhythm and speed of the writing.

The USSR

Russian handwriting has variations, mainly because of the diverse elements that make up that vast country. In 1918 the Russians reformed their writing but still kept the Cyrillic alphabet. Because the Russian alphabet contains quite a few 'hard' letters, the pressure is inclined to be heavy and the writing a little slower than for other European handwriting.

L'unique dictateur Européen e
Les derniers gouvernements totali
- ment contre la demande impe

French handwriting

Yestern hatte ich Besuch.
Freundin Maria aus Has
ist gekommen. Ihr Fle
hatte vier Stunden Vers
Maria

German handwriting

We do not wish to consider
alternatives at this time.

American handwriting

познакомишься со все
я решил отправиться

Russian handwriting: a woman aged 35-36

11

Italy

Italian handwriting has influenced English script since the sixteenth century, and gave the language the word 'italic'. It is flourished and florid, with cursive letters and often embellishments reflecting the Italian temperament.

Italian handwriting: a woman aged about 40

Britain

English handwriting has undergone many changes of style, including the italic, copperplate, secretary hand and Civil Service hand. In the 1930s, Marion Richardson started a particular type of writing which was adopted in schools for a short time. She taught an upright, rounded legible script as she believed it would make for more simply written letters. The handwriting was copybook style and looked immature. It completely suppressed the individuality of the writer. Now, no one style of writing is taught in England. This means that individual traits of personality are allowed to emerge.

English handwriting: Marion Richardson's 1930s script

Handwriting through the ages

There have always been fashions in writing, as can be seen in the following examples:

Thomas Woolvin. Part of the will and signature of a glove-maker, 1730

The writer was literate at a time when few people could read or write. The writing displays the embellishments and scrolls that were fashionable in those days.

John Woolvin, a prison keeper

This is another good example of handwriting from around the 1730s.

13

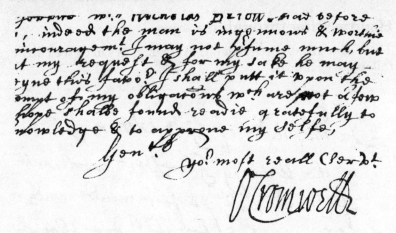

Oliver Cromwell, writing in 1650

Oliver Cromwell tried to simplify the writing of the day, which was mainly Latin. Just after this letter was written, Commonwealth legislators established English as the only language to be used for all domestic purposes in government. When Charles II came to the throne, the 'court hand' (whose flamboyant nature Cromwell detested) was brought back into fashion and it was not until an Act of Parliament was passed that a 'common or legible hand' came into being and Latin began to die out.

Samuel Johnson, 1773

Highly intelligent and unpretentious, this simply made signature with its clear strokes and upright slant points to a man who had no need to exaggerate his importance. His work proved his abilities as the literary giant of the day.

A person's writing can, however, change at different stages of his life, sometimes mirroring changes in his personality and ageing.

T E Lawrence (Lawrence of Arabia)

The small size, speed and formation of this handwriting, simplified and intelligent, shows Lawrence as a highly able and analytical man. He was a brilliant organiser, as his spacing reveals, and there is energy in the pressure. However, the rhythm is not even or consistent, showing inner conflicts.

Regards to John.

Alas : Baker had had to change all his rare wood samples were could only find those few rubl wood . 'Sorry, He has promised come, but I in not there to jo The Press were bad here at first Associations and the Newspaper and as a society : and have

T E Lawrence (second letter, much later)

Lawrence's later writing is even more erratic, with lines entangled and pressure varying. Emotional disturbance can be seen in the undisciplined formation and different size of his letters. It is obvious that there are still many unresolved conflicts in his personality.

Before starting an analysis it is necessary to know the age, sex and nationality of the writer, and to have at least a page of writing and full signature (original).

Age is essential, because some people are old at 20 while others are still young at 70. The sex of the writer is important because everyone has characteristics of both sexes in their physiological make-up. Nationality is necessary because knowing where the writer learnt to write is helpful in assessing characteristics. An original script is best as it will reveal the correct pressure – the libido of the writer.

3. The Three Zones of Handwriting

The three zones are upper, middle and lower.

Personal maturity is reflected in the proportion of upper and lower zones to the middle. Maturity prevents exaggerated deviations – self-limitations are a prerequisite for knowing your own limits and performance. Maturity is seen in a balance between the three zones, the balance between the upper and lower zone signifying reason and instinct. Emphasis of one zone means a loss in others, which points to one-sidedness, and the neglected zones require equal consideration by the analyst.

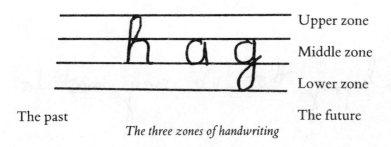

	Upper zone
h a g	Middle zone
	Lower zone

The past   The future

The three zones of handwriting

You will be pleased
to hear that we've got
registrations for Graphology

Well-balanced zones

The upper zone (ascenders)

This symbolises the striving and idealistic qualities of the writer. It shows imagination and vision, the search for perfection, spiritual aspirations, and sometimes the desire for the unobtainable. It can also reveal a lack of self-discipline, a fantasy world, little sense of reality.

When it is exaggeratedly long, it denotes high intellectual or spiritual aims but often without the imagination to carry through ideas. Full upper loops indicate the ability to construct imaginatively.

Exaggerated upper loops

Exaggerated lower loops

Preoccupation with upper zone – lack of realism, keen ethics but lack of emotion and extremely introverted personality

The middle zone

When well balanced and even, it shows a good mind coping with the demands of ego in everyday life, as well as a sense of reality and consideration for others.

When extra large, it shows that the writer's personal sphere dominates everyday life and suggests unstable emotional reactions. It points to a subjective attitude, possibly by someone who is uncritical and highly strung. When parts of the middle-zone letters jut out unnaturally, these are compensatory factors; bursts of self-assertion offsetting self-devaluation.

When the letters of the middle zone are very small, the opposite is the case: the writer is well suited to fit in with the world, but is sometimes susceptible to feelings of inferiority. He may confine himself to a limited field of activity but excels in careful observation of detail. He may underrate himself and his mental attitude, showing only a slight emotional interest in everyday life. The outside world impresses him, but he has less ego than others, possibly lacks enthusiasm, and can be petty-minded and over-scrupulous.

- Actuaries, astronomers, mathematicians, scientists, chemists, opticians and so on are all examples of people whose handwriting is often characterised by a small middle zone.

Well-balanced middle zone

19

te as indicator. The solution
in reaction. Interfering
and thiocyanate.

Large middle zone

independence — on
on her parts and with black
verv. At present she is
ring you both a picture to

that the outcome will be satisfied
or do not agree? In any, e
k needs to be done on both of
med choice can be made between

Small middle zone (two examples)

Preoccupation with middle zone – self-absorption, too much social consideration, no clarity in looking ahead

Exaggerated middle zone

The lower zone (descenders)

This is the sphere of private and primitive instincts, of sexuality, materialism and irrationality, where the material demands of self-preservation are predominant.

Firm strokes and smooth curvatures betoken freedom of movement, plus co-ordination in all bodily movements.

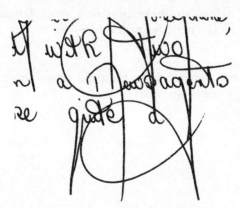

Preoccupation with lower zone – over-active sexual imagination, money-mindedness, materialism, lack of objectivity, poor eye for detail

21

1. An inflated loop shows a money complex, and a strong preoccupation with material matters.

2. A large, long loop is a sign of strong sexual forces. This strength is often connected with outside sports and games, and this type of loop is frequently found in the handwriting of athletes.

3. Lower zone letters without loops and with good pressure show a sense of realism, typified in the highly analytical, probing executive, the kind of person who accepts nothing at face value. It also denotes mental agility.

4. An unfinished loop going to the left points to a mother fixation, emotional immaturity and impressionability.

5. A triangular loop signifies sexual disappointment and aggressive tendencies.

6. A backward 'arcade' (see page 25) reveals an avoidance of responsibility (often sexual) and materialism.

7. A long, full loop shows imagination, erotic fantasy and points to an instinctively active individual.

8. A loop with movement to the right reveals empathy and the ability to work with others.

1

2

3

4

5

6

7

8

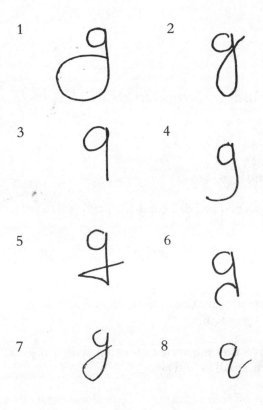

4. Connecting strokes

The four basic connecting strokes are:

1. Arcade
2. Thread
3. Angular
4. Garland

Arcade is arched and cathedral-like, and is seen in the small *n*s and *m*s.

Thread is wavy and snake-like, tapering off into strokes that dissolve.

Angular strokes are firm and rigid, and sometimes inclined to be spiky and pointed.

Garland is a flowing style of writing with a cup-like formation, seen in the small *n*s and *m*s.

The form of connection is of central importance as it expresses the writer's characteristic attitude to life (though not his total personality) and shows his quality of particular adaptability, ie how he bridges the distance between 'I' and 'You'. It shows how the writer approaches his fellow men and whether he links or fails to link himself to the environment (as in the ability to adjust to work, society and life as a whole). It is rare to find only one form in a person's writing.

Handwriting characteristics are difficult to disguise. Copybook is sometimes adopted as a conventional mask, as may be the case with criminals. In a quick and personal form, copybook attaches values to convention and makes a virtue of keeping them.

1. Arcade

This style of writing reveals a lack of flow; the writer adapts, but rarely discloses his inner life. The writing stresses form and deportment, both socially and aesthetically.

The writer may be secretive and watchful, have good structural sense and an artistic sense of proportion. Friendliness is always tested carefully before acceptance.

- Artists, musicians and poets frequently show this style of writing.

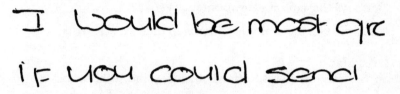

Arcade

2. Thread

With writing that has indefinite linkage lacking in clarity, the 'thread' writer can be all things to all people. In this style, creative personalities flourish. The writer is likely to be elusive, have a psychological talent for understanding people, and a disregard of established forms of convention.

Threads within words
Shows indecisiveness, lack of firm purpose, but flexibility and versatility. In male writing, can indicate a feminine trend.

- Journalists, psychologists, writers, con men, advertising executives.

Thread

3. Angular writing

This style shows a disciplined movement, expressing refusal or inability to adapt, and the writer is more reliable than gracious. Reason and firmness rather than compromise predominate, and the writer will often undertake difficult tasks. He can be hard and unyielding, has will power and a capacity for persistent working methods. Extremely rigid writing can indicate neurotic inner strife and compulsions.

Extremely regular
Destroys the capacity for spontaneity.

- Engineers, technologists, mathematicians, scientists.

Irregular
Shows misguided resolution, obstinacy and stubbornness.

Disconnected
Indicates central conflict within an individual, particularly when seen in the lower zone, revealing disturbance in the erotic or instinctive life.

and also a wvwvvvy
Near week away 8ou
not quite sure where
He asked me to

Angular

Executive ability is seen in angularity, which shows critical faculties, resistance to external pressure, good reasoning powers and objectivity. Simplified script, when combined with medium pressure and right slant, signifies executive qualities.

4. Garland

Smooth, effortless motion signifies genuine adaptation. Adaptability is usually spontaneous. This writer is sociable, easy-going and responsive, but can also be lazy and slightly superficial, and lack firm discipline. In female handwriting, it may reveal over-femininity. It is the handwriting of the unambitious or easily influenced.

Dear Mrs Marne,
you analysed m
handwriting a few
months ago as a re

Garland

5. Slant of Handwriting

The position of the slant should be regarded as the personality desire of the writer, ie a slant to the right indicates extroversion, a slant to the left indicates introversion.

Right slant

The so-called 'normal' slant of handwriting is to the right, indicating an outgoing sociability and desire to move forward and towards the future. It reveals friendly, spontaneous and emotionally demonstrative feelings that do not go to extremes.

• Salesmen, communicators, social workers etc.

When the writing leans too far to the right, it reveals emotional impulsiveness and a lack of control. The writer is influenced by external stimuli to such an extent that his judgement is liable to be faulty and lacking in objectivity. The writer is gregarious and dislikes being on his own for long periods. He may also have sharply contrasting mood variations and sudden likes and dislikes, jumping rapidly from excitement to depression.

Extreme right slant
Shows emotional responsiveness when subjected to the influences of others, uncontrolled irresponsible behaviour and spontaneous feelings of love and hate. There is lack of resistance to internal and external stresses.

Also shows too much dependence upon the outside world, whose influences are yielded to through lack of inner security and stability. Writer unlikely to make objective judgements or good organising decisions.

Such writers must work with others and find it difficult to apply caution or restraint.

fruit & corpses up the hold.
ish friendly seas they softly run,
d-sea blue or shore-sea green,
with the vine & grapes in gold.

Average right slant

Excessive right slant – lack of emotional control

Left slant

A left slant forms a barrier between the writer and the outside world. It often appears during adolescence, when it is due to fear of approaching sexual problems. It is a sign of introversion – an inner state of isolation. The writer is aware of the world, but adopts an artificial approach to others, hiding behind a kind of routine. He is always a little forced, and may be affected and elusive.

There are strong family links resulting in over-protection and love. Writers may also have suffered disappointment and adopted a defensive attitude.

These people work best on their own or with limited supervision.

Extreme left slant

Reveals itself as an expression of emotional life (appears in pubity, especially in girls) showing shrinking from reality and detachment from the outside world. Denotes opposition to everything, and adaptability is alarmingly impeded.

Conflicts in early life experiences have built up negative behaviour and resistance to environmental influences. Often implies an egocentric craving to assume a spurious pose of aloofness and singularity.

Males with pronounced left slant often have strong feelings towards their mothers; females with pronounced left slant inclined to be independent, egotistical and clever with a prevailing opposition to conventional standards of behaviour.

Degree of slant is important in assessing the degree of introversion: handwriting with an extreme slant to the left may show disturbed parental equilibrium leading to an extremely frustrated and disturbed adult.

of this market, and gained man
in the South both with architects
are recently I have been promoted t

Left slant

Dear Madam,
I am writing
may have my
analysed, I a
have my ow
to my make
be very intere

Excessive left slant – introversion

Upright script

This shows a mind which endeavours to meet the outside world and doesn't shrink from it. It reveals reason rather than emotion. Children who write with an upright script like to be recognised for their independence of manner. The upright writer works well on his own, but keeps his distance. He is independent, realistic, impartial, self-reliant and self-sufficient. On the negative side, he can be indifferent, self-contained, pessimistic and unresponsive. He makes a good executive leader and is able to control and maintain discipline, but can be a hard task master. He can command and accept responsibility.

- Managers, lawyers, administrators, civil servants.

which I would like owners
to move to let me out.

herewith, several small recent samples of
along with some signatures of varying
excellent working relationship, so I feel

Upright script (two examples)

6. Introversion and Extroversion

Apart from the revelations of slant, look at the formation of *w* and *d* (especially *w*). When the end stroke of *w* turns inwards or backwards, or when *d* turns in a similar way instead of finishing on the endstroke downwards, this is an indication of introversion. Pay attention to children's handwriting, as the tendency can be eradicated.

Introverted sign in d *and* w

This formation and right slant
The writer is an extrovert.

Variable formation
Implies partial introversion.

Introversion

Positive characteristics
Analytical
Imaginative
Attentive to detail
Methodical
Orderly
Patient
Careful
Reflective

Negative characteristics
Self-conscious
Self-analytical
Shy
Lacks confidence
Sensitive to atmosphere
and environment
Inhibited
Possibly suffers inward
anxiety

Extroversion

Positive characteristics
Self-confident
Friendly
Sociable
Enthusiastic
Warm
Active
Persuasive
Has sales ability

Negative characteristics
Careless
Impatient
Overlooks details
Over-hasty in making
decisions
Impulsive
Lacks planning ability
Lacks organising ability
Reckless

7. General Layout of Handwriting

Well-arranged writing

This denotes intellectual order, a wide mental range and clarity of judgement, as well as good organisation and co-ordination. There is an intelligent disposition of time and space which comes from a good sense of conception and distribution. The writer shows orderliness, a desire to think carefully, to survey, organise and elucidate. He has a rapid grasp of situations, but tends to put logic and orderliness before natural instincts and spontaneity. He is noted for prompt decision-making.

Did I tell you about
group which meets regula
We met originally on a
course at Knuston Hall nea
Only 3 of us meet now,

Well-arranged writing

Badly arranged writing

This reveals a fertile, spontaneous mind but no ability to plan or prepare. The writer has no appreciation of time or space, and could be in a constant muddle. He is likely to be indecisive.

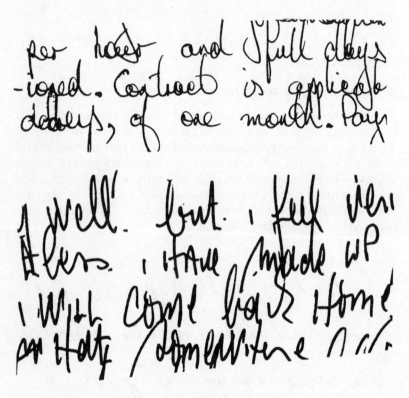

Badly arranged writing (two examples)

Spacing

Clear spacing between letters, words and lines indicates a state of mind – orderly or erratic.

Spacing between lines

Well-spaced lines are accompanied by rhythmic balance showing clearmindedness, orderliness and the power to elucidate. Reveals an executive type – scholastic, abstract-thinking, intellectual and skilled; is able to survey situations – has discerning and critical faculties and is a born organiser. May lack spontaneity, as the writer judges from a distance. Is likely to be an all–round liberal, self-assured and expansive.

Overlarge spacing between lines
Shows isolation or detachment from social or psychological relationships, lack of spontaneity, and reasoning power at the cost of directness and spontaneity.

Extremely large spacing
Indicative of intellectual pride and snobbery leading to melancholy and isolation.

Over-large spacing between lines

Narrow spacing
Reveals no feeling for privacy. Indicator of insecurity, unsure ego and craving for contact. Shows lack of reserve, warmth and spontaneity, obtrusiveness; also lack of sense of distance and distinction, tact and clearmindedness. Very narrow letters and extreme compaction reveal anxiety and/or obsession.

Insufficient spacing (crowding)
Impulse dominates intellect.

Narrow spacing between lines

Irregular spacing

Denotes emotional instability. Writers possess varying degrees of clearmindedness, and periods of reserve, caution and calculation. They may be artists, or people who deal with hard facts in an imaginative or intuitive way.

Unbalanced spacing
Indicates erratic sociability.

Overlapping lines
Reveals difficulty in surveying situations with judgement.

Irregular spacing between lines

Spacing between words

Good word spacing
Shows judgement and clear thinking.

Good spacing between words (two examples)

Wide spacing
Often starts in adolescence – implies criticism of other people; sometimes indicates conceit, isolation, reserve, caution or shyness and inhibition.

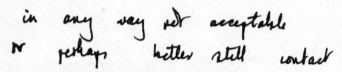

Wide spacing between words

Narrow spacing
Writers are impelled by direct action rather than consideration and reasoning. They lack reserve, are impatient and self-confident – self-contained units generating immediate power and action.

Narrow spacing between words

Spacing between letters

Gaps
Signify irritation, lack of adaptability, fear of the future, spontaneity and isolation.

Overlapping letters
Denote unchecked impulsiveness and self-identification with others' reactions.

Narrow spacing between letters

Size

Size of handwriting expresses the size of personal self-esteem (which can be spontaneous in the case of nobility, royalty etc).

Medium and normal

Balanced writing invariably belongs to the person who neither over- nor underestimates himself with regard to others. He usually likes to conform to normal standards. Self-confidence and the ability to adapt to reality are equally distributed.

However, enough detail was l

esentation, to encourage the appl

Medium and average size

Large writing

Large writing strongly reflects subconscious feelings. It is found in children, whose sense of reality is too under-developed to realise the limitations of their ego.

Since the late 1960's, the n an unaltering diet of their national team. The ba

Large size

Large writing with large spacing and no right margin
Indicates self-esteem and is the sign of a spendthrift.

Excessively large handwriting
Implies preoccupation with personal sphere in everyday life; the writer overrates the importance of self in social life.

People with large handwriting have a desire to live life on a rich scale. They may need to put on a display or have a habit of expansive gestures and movements (such as actors, orators etc). They need recognition and have a tendency to strike poses and for staginess. They can be independent, bold, generous and enthusiastic, but also lacking in objectivity, boastful, easily distracted and poorly disciplined.

Excessively large

Small writing

These writers are more likely to channel their energies into thought than action. They are intelligent, analytical and have a distaste for boasting. Small writing is found among scientists, philosophers and religious people, but beware of lurking arrogance as opposed to genuine unpretentiousness.

Extremely small handwriting shows feelings of inferiority and low self-esteem, but these can be difficult to identify.

Small writing reveals the faculty of observation: concentration comes easily to these writers, and they are critical, clever and often academic. Conscientious, reserved and able to husband personal resources, they opt intentionally for understatement. They often possess business acumen and executive ability.

On the negative side, they can be petty, over-scrupulous, pedantic and unable to see things on a large scale.

Small size (two examples)

With large spacing
The sign of a critical observer.

With narrow spacing
Indicates parsimony.

43

Minute writing
Points to an inferiority complex, and possibly hypochondria.

Minute writing

Alignment

Ascending
Shows optimism, excitement, enthusiasm, elation (constant or temporary), an increasing urge for activity, a fighting spirit, ambition, a desire for communication, and impulsiveness.

No right margin
Implies impulsiveness and thoughtless courage.

Descending
Shows depression, pessimism, criticism, despondency, ill-health, tiredness, weakness and languidness.

Dirty, pasty, neglected letter forms
Indicative of bad digestion.

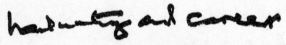

Pasty writing

Small letters, low pressure, slack connective strokes, left tendency, signature to lower left
Signals dangerous depression.

In fast writing
Shows concentration on communication.

Horizontal
A feature of reliability. Writer is likely to be balanced, with a sense of direction, showing firmness and the ability to maintain drive and complete an undertaking. He is not easily deflected, and shows self-control and equanimity (either from steadfastness or unapproachability).

Undulating

A possible indicator of unreliability (compare with 'thready'). Shows indecision, hesitancy, inclination to avoid commitment, lack of stability, preference for compromise, lack of purpose and a crafty or diplomatic disposition. Writer will be over-sensitive, impressionable, and easily swayed by outside influences. Disappointments will produce insecurity, and an unsteady frame of mind may come either from great excitability or lack of inner firmness and stability.

Convex arc

Writer is quick to be enthusiastic (or ambitious) but lacks persistence.

⌣ ⌣ arrangement.

Concave arc

Writer is prone to sinking mood, then recovers spirit in a successful fight against pessimism. Goes through hard times or physical weakness, but has the mental energy to stick it out.

⌢ ⌢ arrangement.

Line ending compressed and curved downward

Shows improvidence and wasteful use of time and energy; lack of organisation and foresight (will dawdle or rush, is spendthrift or miserly, spends too long over preliminaries or will rush to finish).

Drooping at right margin

Indicates possible financial difficulties and lack of economy (but not necessarily in the case of fast writing).

Ascending lines

A sign of temporary financial embarrassment.

Extreme variability

Writer is hypersensitive and moody.

Initial letter higher than the rest or step-like descending line

Shows fight against weariness supported by strong feelings of responsibility.

Last word letter higher than the rest or step-like descending line
Attempt to be impulsive.

Broken or staggering (erratic)
Points to incoherent thought and action; writer cannot think straight, goes to pieces.

Writing above printed line
Writer may be enthusiastic, is lacking in sense of reality, and independent.

Writing below printed line
Writer has a strong sense of reality but is devoid of enthusiasm, and concerned with material things.

8. Pressure

This is the domain of drive, energy and libido. The choice of nib is of paramount importance and when assessing the amount of pressure used by a writer it is essential to study ballpoint by magnifying glass. Measurement of unconscious dynamic urges is shown in pressure. It does not necessarily indicate volitional energies but accumulated energies in general (whether or not they are transformed into active achievement).

Heavy (normally downstroke)
Shows tendency towards conscientiousness, willpower and steadiness in achieving objectives. Would accept a challenge and prefers direct action to contemplation. May be emotionally irritable and aggressive, with desire to have own way irrespective of consequences.

Heavy pressure

Pressure with regularity and speed
Shows independent nature. Writer is self-willed and efficient.

Uneven pressure

Energies are employed erratically and the writer does his best only when under scrutiny.

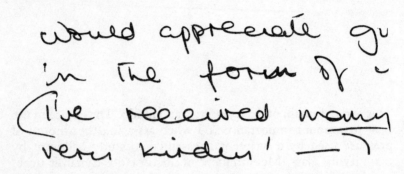

Uneven pressure

Medium pressure

The majority of writers are in this group. Varying pressure can reflect mood variations.

Medium pressure

Light pressure

Can denote apathy.

Light pressure

Slow writing with heavy pressure

Reveals calmness, coolness, self-control, caution and a sense of economy; occasionally indicates indecisiveness and self-consciousness.

9. Regularity and Rhythm

Regularity, pressure and speed indicate functional energies – their intensity, economy and scope. These features are important for judging the mode of work and scale of achievements. *Regular* is when the size of small letters, the writing angle, distance between and height of downstroke, and line direction are constant. Reveals economical use of energies and signifies relationship of will to emotions and impulses.

Rhythmic (harmonious and even distribution) is when the same writing tendency is maintained throughout.

Regularity and rhythm are harmonious

Regular rhythm (produced by an act of will)

A tendency to regularity can lead to compulsive behaviour: the writer is able to regulate the energies of mind and impulses by an act of will.

Positive characteristics	Negative characteristics
Self-control	Lack of vitality
Self-discipline	Spontaneity
Willpower (enhanced in	Personality
emotional types)	Feelings and emotions
Endurance, concentration	Imagination
Perseverance, balanced	Excitability
personality	Capacity to change
Reliability, sense of harmony	Pedantry
Sense of duty, singularity of	Monotony
purpose	
Regular mind	

Controlled

Excessive regularity

Shows lack of impulses – strong self-discipline suppressing expression of personality.

Excessive regularity

Rigid at cost of speed and elasticity
The writer is rigid, automatic, pedantic, colourless; spontaneity and emotions are low; compulsion is evident.

Increasing regularity and insufficient spacing
Signifies a neurotic disposition.

Evenness
Shows a degree of objectivity or emotional excitability; also balance and harmony, ie the writer produces like things in like distance.

He is emotionally calm, difficult to excite, possesses inner harmony, equanimity and tranquillity. Not easily provoked or irritated.

Irregular rhythm

Emotion and spontaneity prevail over discipline and rationality.

Irregular rhythm

Positive characteristics	Negative characteristics
Emotional sensitivity (or rich emotional life)	Excitability
	Spontaneity
Imagination and external impressions have great power to influence	Not bound by tradition
	Not bound by conventions

52

Liveliness of feelings
Multiple and changing purposes
Capacity to change
Changing moods
Many-sided interests
Impulsiveness
Shunning of routine

Nervous instability
Lack of self-discipline
Lack of steadiness and tidiness
Easy to influence, uneven working capacity, absent-mindedness
Reactions incalculable

Middle zone height fluctuates considerably
Shows extreme sensitivity (confirm elsewhere in script).

Greatly varying slant
Writer is impulsive.

No pressure
Points to instability, emptiness.

Wealth of individual forms, convincing rhythm and pressure
Shows creative power or unbalanced self-reliance, lack of restraint and inhibition, mixed impulses and intellect.

Rhythmic
A sign of calmness and equilibrium – sometimes indifference.

Unrhythmic writing

This is an indicator of a high degree of emotionality, abrupt changes of temper, a passionate character and instability of the nervous system.

Uneven rhythm
The rhythm is uneven when the writing shows unexpected oscillations in the intervals between words, lines or letters, in pressure, writing angle, or size of letters, and great difference of height. The writer will be restless and excitable, highly susceptible to impressions, easily influenced and lacking in harmony and balance.

10. Degree of Connection

Disconnected writing

As a group, such writers are associated with individualism, isolation, and the desire to live a separate and detached life. The mental process is full of new ideas, provided the imaginary connection is working well – otherwise the 'brain waves' become directionless 'brain spray'. Ideas can germinate.

Writers are unsociable and have difficulty in fitting in.

Just a line to let you that I will be returning to

Disconnected writing

inform them of the work involved in

b) To assess the applicants, as to th

the job in question.

Connected writing

Positive characteristics	Negative characteristics
Inventiveness	Lack of forethought
Planning	Lack of security
Intuitive thinking	Lack of logical reasoning
Productive observation	Lack of concentration and
Individualism	method
Intellectual initiative	Lack of willpower
Quick grasp and insight	Lack of empathy
Critical perception	Lack of capacity for constant
Inspiration	practical or moral behaviour
Emotional sensitivity	Stubbornness
	Moodiness

Slightly disconnected writing
Points to uncertainty and sometimes indecision, germination of ideas within limited field.

Little connected, light pressure and round forms
Shows a good natural memory.

Connected final letters
A sign of acquired adaptability.

In lower zone
Shows lack of ability to establish relationships, and loneliness (see 'lower zone', page 21).

Pronounced gaps in words and fluctuating pressure
This shows sensitivity.

Frequent and large intervals inside words
The writer suffers from excessive blackouts, loss of memory, and has difficulty in mastering frequent and distracting ideas.

Breaking individual letters into parts
A sign of a disturbed personality.

Breaks in vertical up- and down-strokes
The writer may have heart trouble.

Fragmented writing with no up-strokes
Shows a lack of connection with the world. The writer is eccentric, neurotic, egocentric, an introvert and a social recluse.

11. Speed

Speed is indicated by fluency, overstrokes (dotting of *i*, crossing of *t*-bar) to the right of a letter, writing which slopes to the right, word end strokes extended to the right, connected writing, angle or thread connection and ascending lines.

The tempo of writing corresponds to the tempo of a personality – this is important in detecting forgery, which must be done slowly.

Writes slowly
Can become heated and react violently in argument. Energies tend to be stored up and can erupt quickly.

Quick writing

Speed – quick

Positive characteristics
Tendency towards
extroversion
Adaptability
Spontaneity
Quick thinking and mental
grasp
Objectivity
Impatience, pertinence
Lack of exaggerated self-
observation
Need for change
Need for stimulation
Topical enthusiasm
Vivacity
Intelligence
Zeal
Agility
Interest
Initiative
Energy and vitality
Impulsiveness
Ambition
Elasticity
Liveliness
Purposefulness

Negative characteristics
Could lack analytical approach
Could lack profound
penetration
Could lack concentration
Could be influenced
Absent-mindedness
Superficial manner
Lack of planning ability
Lack of steadiness
Lack of definite thinking
Excitability
Rashness
Aimlessness
Unreliability
Neglect of detail
Shallowness
Hastiness
Mechanical routine

Insufficient spacing
Shows poor judgement.

Lack of pressure
Points to increased lack of self-control.

Connected writing
Signifies need for human contact.

Well-formed middle lengths
Signifies need for variety.

Poorly written letter forms
The writer is careless, over-hasty and forgetful.

Irregular speed
Shows impatience, especially with slow people.

Slow writing

This is characterised by uneven strokes and a lack of trimness and smoothness.

looking for the handwriting of someone who isn't very

Speed – slow

Positive characteristics
Steadiness
Level-headedness
Contemplativeness
Thoughtfulness
Carefulness
Thrift
Self-control (moral or intellectual)
Balance
Considerateness
Circumspection
Preciseness

Negative characteristics
Passivity
Hesitancy
Adventurous swindler
Cautiousness
Phlegm
Laziness
Indecision
Inner tension
Irresponsibility
Snobbery

Weak pressure
This is a sign of apathy and indecisiveness.

Descending lines
Point to depression.

Slurs and omissions

Show laziness and fatigue. When contradicted by features and
initiative and energy, this indicates that the writer holds back and
calculates every word; control becomes a disguise. When found
in mature writing, the writer is 'writing conscious', concerned
with style (eg painters and those with artistic minds).

The philosophy that "salesmen
made" has been a bone of
almost all types of people can
in past generations; and be
or rejected according to point
that nowadays when we liv

Speed – average

12. The *T*-Bar

Positioning of the *t*-bar is of vital importance as it indicates such factors as leadership and control of others, but beware of diagnosing lack of self-confidence when a lower bar is caused by a following connection. Take note of the capital *T* as well.

Connecting *i* dots, accents, and *t*-bars with following or preceding letters points to an outstanding faculty for logical and intellectual combination in the writer, and usually an ability for scientific research.

- Writers, artists, lawyers, psychologists, people with intellectual ability.

All the following placings apply to *any slant*.

Left position

-ι

This denotes caution, uncertainty, procrastination, depression, feelings of inferiority, lack of essential drive and zest on the part of the writer. He may possess leadership potential but be disinclined to use it fully.

Assorted *t*-bars

ƛ   Caution, restraint, meditation

ƭ   Lack of confidence, obedience, tendency to be subservient or subordinate, complaisance

ι–   (Long, medium *t*-bar, detached) Activity, enterprise and thoughts that run ahead of the action. The writer will accept challenges, is prepared to meet new projects, is stimulated by others' ideas and will never stagnate

t   Even application of energy

t   Concentration

-*t*-   Quickness of thinking, enterprise, thoughts run ahead of action, haste

t   (Long *t*-bar to the right) Desire for power, desire to protect, authority, fatherly spirit, patronising. The writer can take responsibility and exercise protective measures towards those coming within his orbit of control, and is able to solve problems

t   (*Long and thin*) Impulsiveness, but lack of stamina

t   Aggression, ambition, quarrelsome tendency

t   Egoism

t   Grabbing, pocketing, greed for money and material goods, profit motive, rascal

t   (Bar sharpening) Malicious criticism, hypersensitivity, sarcasm

t   (Thin bar becoming thicker) Physical violence and cruelty, domination

t   (Low *t*-bar) Depression and no opinion of self; sulkiness, resentment, nonco-operation

t   (If thin bar) Weak health

t   A longing to be at the top, bossiness, ambition, idealism, high-flying dreams, neglect of realities

t   A sense of fun

t   Awkwardness, obstinacy, persistence, pig-headedness, sulkiness, aggressiveness, coercion, lack of tolerance, blackmail tendency, fanatical objection to any interference

ƒ   Literary ability, but also seen in female sexual deviants

ƴ   Protects independence in fanatical and pugnacious fashion

ɗ   Demonstrative happiness, pride in achievements of self and family, toughness, thoroughness

ƒ   Meanness, inhibition

ƈ   Vanity, sensitivity to criticism, emotional

ſ   Quick, ready liar, automatic and superficial friendliness

ʎ   (*Upside down*) Treats facts the same way

t t (Letters joined) Natural problem-solving, highly valuable in all branches of commerce and industry, mental gymnastics (crossword puzzles, chess problems)

l   (No *t*-bar) Impatience, no acceptance of responsibility, impulsiveness, lack of real objective, drifting, physical weakness and sometimes in consequence laziness and indifference, carelessness, lack of consideration, unconventionality, considers himself different.

t-bar *connected with following letter* Clever mind, grasps things quickly, easily understood, ability for scientific precision and research

t-bar connected backwards Diplomatic impenetrability, sharp intellect, critical attitude

t-bar connected farther ahead (or back) Ability to connect and associate remote facts or events

13. *I*-Dots

Low
Writer is realistic, practical and down-to-earth.

High
Indicates characteristics of planning, surveying and enquiring.

Correct placing
Denotes accuracy – an eye for detailed work

- Surgeons, dentists, fine mechanics.

To the right
Shows enterprise and fast-flowing thoughts.

To the left
Denotes hesitation and caution.

Low with a left slant
The writer is likely to be extremely cautious and reserved with a practical trend. He may also show attention to detail and have a retentive memory but little imagination; or he may be basically cautious and reserved with a practical trend and inclination but able to display action and enthusiasm.

High with a left slant
Some writers are reserved, very enquiring or even inquisitive, able in the areas of planning and survey, and extremely cautious. Others are less cautious and characterised by accuracy, some reserve, marked enquiry and inquisitiveness, planning and surveying ability, and imagination and vision.

In other writers, these attributes are linked with action and movement.

Low and upright
Writers are likely to be practical, realistic and cautious; they are highly accurate with marked judgement.

- Accountants, systems analysts, programmers, personnel officers.

I-dot joining next word
Writers are active, independent and realistic (eg workers requiring speed, accuracy and judgement).

High and upright
Writers possess inquisitive, enquiring minds and are basically independent. They display judgement but may hold back due to cautionary factors.

Low with a right slant
I-dot forward of handwriting, the writer displays adaptability but there is a degree of caution in the practical and realistic sense – a slight measure of delay before things move forward. He can often be characterised by accuracy, realism, and positive qualities.

With some, there is impatience, restlessness and a desire for extreme action. They seek after goals, show a propensity for new enterprises and marked realistic and practical adaptability. (Most executives show these trends.)

High with a right slant
Writers are enquiring, inquisitive and adaptable. There is a link between action and planning. They may be cautious, but only in the sense of applying careful observation.

Some are enquiring, inquisitive, accurate and exact. Their planning and surveying abilities are well co-ordinated.

Well-placed *i*-dot
Signifies forward vision. The writer realises possible contingencies and warns of approaching difficulties.

I-dot missing
Shows indifference, laziness, impatience, lack of respect for the reader and forgetfulness (but check elsewhere in the script).

Heavy dot close to top
Indicates subservience, and a deeply depressed mind.

Arrowlike
Sign of speed and observation.

High flying
Denotes lack of accuracy – high-minded ideals.

Cube (square dot)
Indicative of vitality, and sometimes brutality.

Horizontal stroke
A sign of hypersensitivity.

Right-facing arc
This is the 'watching eye' – an important indication of highly developed observation faculty.

Comma form
Shows critical intellect.

Small circle
Indication of slow speed, desire to be different (often used by architects and designers).

Dot connected to next letter
Mature; writer is rapid in thought and very intelligent. He has organising and co-ordinating ability as well as ability for detailed work and scientific research.

Dot connected backwards to last letter
Indicates diplomatic impenetrability, sharp intellect and critical attitude.

Dot connected to first letter of next word
Shows intuition, constructiveness, planning, deductive thinking, vision and foresight.

Dot connected to last letter of word
A sign of organising ability and integration.

Dot connected farther ahead (or back) than next letter
Writer is able to connect and associate remote facts or events.

14. Punctuation

In general, a dot registers some sort of retention. Complete omission of the dot shows carelessness, negligence and a lack of consideration.

The full stop expressed as a circle indicates a desire for attention.

Excessive punctuation (much use of hyphens and underlining) points to insistence; the writer is snobbish, vain, affected and places a foolish emphasis on his own views.

Overlong commas are a sign of over-emphasis of principles.

15. Signatures

Official and private signatures may differ (possibly owing to different ethics). The family name or surname is representative of the social and collective element; the forename (initial) represents the more private and intimate side. Examples are shown on pages 71–72.

Signature completely identified with script
Writer is natural and unpretentious, showing unchanged behaviour in both business and private life. He has equipoise, is even-natured and lacks self-concern, self-consciousness and veneer. He can be complacent, but also objective when considering own faults and virtues.

Signature smaller than script
Statement of unimportance of self. Writer appears more modest than he actually is; assumes role which is not a genuine expression of self. Is mild, lacking in force, unconcerned with other people's opinion of himself. Can be self-deprecating, servile, sometimes lacking in dignity; making a deliberate attempt to represent self as inferior (protective measure). May be sensitive and unwilling to show full potential. Tends to undervalue self (though humility may be artificial). A sign of introversion: strong inferiority feelings are submerged.

Signature larger than script
Points to an individual who is more self-reliant in private sphere than openly; demonstrates wish to over-compensate for lack of self-reliance in social intercourse. Shows pride, forcefulness, desire to be recognised as an important figure; possesses greater self-esteem than he admits. Wishes to impress. Larger signature suggests stature and prestige, and indicates the potential of the young who show ambition.

Left slant of signature, right script

Reveals repression of normal affectionate and sociable nature, a brake on natural responsiveness (can be result of domestic problems, unnatural atmosphere).

General extroversion used only for effect; in reality writer is naturally reserved – adopted in order to adjust to situations. Can show inner conflict.

Right slant of signature, left script

Denotes wish to represent warm and affectionate front, which is a veneer. Can apply to demonstrative and effusive individuals who are actually unemotional – sometimes associated with schemes of a secretive nature. If reserve is main characteristic of external behaviour, be wary – points to possible inner conflict.

Clear without embellishments

Shows moral courage, personality without concealment, social conscientiousness, possibly pedantry.

Not congruent with body of writing

Indicates desire to take on disguise for self-protection; fantasy at odds with reality.

Illegible

Trademark of routine (eg business people, officials); sometimes reveals shirking of responsibility.

Capital is smaller than other letters

A sign of self-devaluation – (of personal pronoun).

Highly exaggerated capitals and signature

Shows inferiority feelings giving rise to defensive behaviour pattern; veneer, false pride, pretentiousness.

Very flourished

Mark of ostentation, vanity, love of display. Lasso-like flourish shows desire to attract attention. Writer is very self-assertive, with desire to control; resents interference.

Signature with lasso flourish

Flourish with left tendency
Indicates guilt feelings, originating in imagination.

Drooping end stroke
Shows a dwindling of energy, a dying out movement.

Forenames and family names balanced
Signifies harmonious interaction of private and social roles.

Over-emphasis of family name
Expresses family pride, feelings of prestige, a preoccupation with status and power, and sacrificing of private and intimate life. Narcissistic urge on part of writer to attract attention; importance of private life extinguished in favour of social considerations.

Over-emphasis of forename
In married women, denotes a preference for the unmarried state.

Different slant of fore- and last names
Points to strife within the family or aversion to own upbringing (especially in women). There is conflict between private and social life.

Encircled signature
A sign of anxiety, the desire to enclose and shelter self. Writer suffers from feelings of persecution and withdrawal.

Capital letter of signature deleted by end stroke
Indicates heavy disappointment, a critical attitude towards ego and suicidal tendencies.

Lasso under name
Denotes calculated cleverness. Writer is charming or sly, able to capture others (found in pickpockets).

Strokes extended left
In upper zone this points to intellectual hang-ups from the past; middle zone – remembered feelings; lower zone – relates to past material and erotic matters.

Central placing on line
This indicates a degree of inhibition, avoidance of the outside world. Can conversely indicate a desire to be in the middle of things (the opposite).

Extreme right placing
Writer is impatient – consumed by nervous energy.

Extreme left placing
Shows withdrawal, a high degree of inner isolation.

With left slant
Points to suicidal tendencies.

Left and right strokes in forenames and last names
A sign of schizophrenia.

Signature characteristics
Large – egotism
Small – inferiority feelings
Underlined – self-importance
Cramped and narrow – shyness
Large and bold – ambition
Tall and narrow – meanness

Merging of initials with family name
Points to ego emphasis if pressure is heavy.

Pressure
An expression of passion and energy.

Ascending signature
An indicator of success and ambition.

Descending signature
Shows discouragement. Writer may suffer from fatigue, illness or depression.
   A step-like signature shows a struggle against depression.

Dot at end of signature
There is an impulse to come to an end, to cut off; used by the fastidious, it also shows suspicion.

Dot at beginning of signature
Points to deliberate concentration before starting.

Dot appearing arbitrarily
Shows inhibitive mechanism is at work.

Underlining
A sign of ego emphasis and self-confidence. Writer is firm, determined, with a sense of own importance. Able to take responsibility.

Clear-cut and firmly drawn
Shows poise and firmness.

Extension of initial letter below signature
A sign of conceit (and often found in aristocracy).

Examples

1. Strong sense of self-protection – often a sign of would-be suicide – bid to keep the world at bay

2. Aggressive – forward-thinking but erratic; sense of own importance

Joy Smith

3. Unpretentious but poor form level

Michael Merlin

4. Mentally agile – ego drive – intuitive – manipulative

Keith James

5. Open – reliable – no veneer.

(signature)

6. Ostentatious – vain – seeker after attention – poor taste

Anthony John

7. Skilled executive – objective – clever – good judgement

E. Clegg.

8. Lack of self-esteem – inferiority feelings

Signatures of famous people

Charles Dickens

Dickens had a habit of underscoring his signature in a bizarre manner. It reveals his ego drive and also shows an attempt to impress. The amount of energy he expended on this underlining indicates his vitality, but this curious idiosyncracy tells much about his character. The encircling of the initial letter of his first name is a sign of inhibition and dislike for the first part of his life and his early and formative years; their influence was still strong within him and even fame could not alter it.

Sigmund Freud

Freud had a bold, quick, right-slanted signature revealing confidence, energy and mental agility. The long downstrokes show his ability to probe the unconscious and there is a touch of the old Austro-Germanic Gothic script in the angular lines and strokes.

When he became world famous, he dropped the 'Sigmund' and signed himself simply as 'Freud'.

Salvador Dali

The eccentric artist shows creativity and originality in the formation of his signature, which is more like a picture than writing and symbolises his unique talent. There is sensuality in the thick, pasty strokes and the unusual spirals at the beginning are often seen in the writing of people who suffer from feelings of persecution.

Hailsham of Marylebone

An aristocratic ego is displayed in the flourishes and whirls of this signature. The writer is full of status and prestige, and he wants the world to know it. This is a good example of aristocratic handwriting from the past.

Michael Heseltine

The high upper loops of this signature show rampant ambition. The shaky lines and poor rhythm reveal a disturbed nervous system, and an aggressive arrogance can be seen in the varying slant, to right and left – a sign that the writer is frequently pulled in several directions at once and is unpredictable.

```
I hope I can count on your support on
Polling Day.
```

Albert Einstein

Modest and simple, this signature signifies a man who is intellectual but unassuming. The small, neat script reveals his ability to eliminate non-essentials and the thread-like strokes are often seen in the handwriting of people who have a psychological talent for dealing with people.

16. Signs of Unreliability

Confused thinking is seen in erratic spacing between lines, words and letters; letters entangled in the next line and inflated capitals. Crossing out or going over letters more than once is a sign of neuroticism.

Large writing is symbolic of an exaggerated ego, and shows a bid for attention. It can also be a compensation for an inferiority complex brought on by feelings of inadequacy, revealing a preoccupation with status and position.

Varying slant

A varying slant reveals that the writer, although versatile and quick thinking, rapidly loses interest and is erratic and mercurial. The *a*s and *o*s open at the top show talkativeness and the inability to keep a secret.

Inflated capitals

Inflated or exaggerated capital letters are seen in the handwriting of people who love the limelight and enjoy plenty of attention.

The egoist

Huge embellishments in writing are a sign of the egoist who seeks to be the centre of his circle (pop stars, TV personalities etc), the weak-willed and those with an inferiority complex. They indicate that the writer is more interested in impressing his personality than conveying a message. Inflated capitals can also point to neurotic tendencies as they demonstrate a desire that is narcissistic in its bid for attention. It is a weakness seen in the handwriting of many criminals.

Unreliability can be deduced from a wavering baseline and poor *t*-bar crossing. Letters that are rounded at the top (*m*s and *n*s) and varying slant show subjectivity due to immaturity; varied slants indicate weak will and indecision.

Left tendencies

Left-tending strokes in capitals indicate deceitfulness, when seen with frequent long loops and reaching too far to the left. They are an unmistakable sign of unreliability and deceit; this may not always be criminal deceit – it can be emotional, and indicates a fair amount of vanity on the part of the writer.

17. Signs of Reliability

Signs of reliability are shown in a straight baseline; mental maturity is seen in angles and letters that are firm and well formed, determination in a strong *t*-bar crossing. The less inconsistent a person is, the less likely it is that he will be at the mercy of fluctuating moods – therefore rhythmic writing is a sign of stability and balance.

Well-organised thinking is seen in well-arranged lines, good spacing between words and a clear, legible script. Either right-slanted or slightly upright script shows reliability, good head control, sociability and objectivity.

18. Signs of Stress

These are seen in the following characteristics:

Unexpected breaks in letters
Exaggerated gaps within words
Large spaces between words; letters varying in size
Many amendments to letters (sign of neuroticism)
Extreme left slant
Heavy pressure which fluctuates
Shaky strokes (unless caused by illness, alcoholism or drugs)
Any omission of letters within words
Resting dots between words or letters

Printed script

This is often a mask for emotional disturbances. It should not be analysed – especially for personnel selection – without a sample of normal handwriting. Disconnected printed script can hide emotional, social and even mental difficulties.

ACCOUNTS, THIS WENT DOWN
I WAS THEN ASKED TO NO
BASIS. THIS LOOKED VERY GO
WAY IT TURNED OUT WAS

Printed script

19. Criminal Signs and Symbols

There are many faces of dishonesty: mental, criminal and emotional. We are dealing here with conscious dishonesty for the purpose of self-interest, which can be revealed by negative traits in handwriting.

The following characteristics are signposts to deceit, hypocrisy and dishonesty. However, at least five of these traits should be seen in a sample of handwriting before a firm conclusion is reached that the writer is too dishonest to be taken on as an employee; one or two traits are merely warning signals.

Variable slant: Moody
Touching up of letters/figures: Neurotic
Wide, flat *m*s: Bluffer. Can also show deceit and hypocrisy.
Uneven pressure: Erratic behaviour
Pasty writing: Sensuality
Small *a* and *o* open at base: Cardinal sign of dishonesty
Weak *t*-bars: Weak will
Difference between script and signature: Taken with other
    signs could indicate dishonesty or different ethics
Highly flourished or exaggerated capitals and letters: Show-off
Illegibility: Evasive
Printed script: Often used by criminals for concealment
Dots appearing inside words: An inhibitive factor. Can be a
    sign of shyness or deceit
Left-tending strokes in capitals: Deceit
Enrolments (scrolled flourishes) of letters: Vanity
Flattened 'arcade', illegible signature
Large writing ending in 'thread'
Left-turning strokes which should turn right
Capital *I* or figures made in form of £ or $ (dollar) sign.

Split letters: Lying

there is not a silly

Split letters

money will be there

Dots between words

20. Numerals

It is often interesting to compare normal numbers with those used for writing amounts of money on cheques and bills, which are often larger, denoting a concern with material values.

Smoothly written numerals
Show a serious and sober attitude towards material values. When small, sharp and concise, indicate routine involvement in and concentration on financial matters.

● Accountants, executives, mathematicians, physicists.

Indistinct numerals
These allow different interpretations. Can point to negligently indifferent or neurotic attitude to material values, sometimes a blurring of monetary issues in favour of writer; appear occasionally in blackmail letters.

Amended numerals
Indicate a neurotic reaction, financial anxiety and problems – especially if, for example, 'money' figures are altered but the date untouched.

Decorative numerals
Writer indulges in daydreams, turning away from realistic aspect of material values. He is clumsy (especially in fluent writing) and poor at maths, with no concept of numbers. Shows neglect of the practical and pettiness in material matters.

21. The Meaning of Ink

The colour of ink and style of pen is personal to each writer.

A sensitive writer often prefers a fountain pen, as do many executives.

The use of different coloured inks, especially to underline words, indicates that the writer is a fool.

Blues
The colour of inspiration, showing harmonious understanding, loyalty, concern with spiritual matters and sincerity.

Royal Blue
Writer is seldom depressed. The colour is purposely chosen. Women especially seem to delight in this colour as it suggests femininity and affection.

Blue/Black
Universal business colour, indicating a masculine mind. Writers are conventional, with no desire to be exceptional or to show out-of-the-ordinary personality.

Washy Blue
Writer is banal and unimaginative.

Blacks
A serious colour contrast to blue – much more dominant.

Heavy Black/Pale Brown
When used with a broad nib, points to a bold type who means to be noticed. Indicates power, force, seriousness towards life in general. Used by students, designers, business people who are going to make their mark or have already done so.

With a thin nib, used by artistic groups (writers, artists,

musicians, poets). Denotes seriousness, sometimes depression.
Writers can be hypersensitive.

Red
A sign of ambition; generosity and affection; strong likes and
dislikes. Can indicate the pedant or know-all: the pompous
school-master, accountant, lecturer. Red is the 'professional'
colour, giving just that shade of difference for those who want to
be different.

Green
The writer likes to be apart and distinguished. Can show possible
inferiority complex where linked with copy book form. Used by
young people connected with the artistic field. It is a symbol of
harmony, adaptability, versatility, and mental development
extending beyond the normal.

Violet
Especially when combined with coloured paper, shows a
keenness to be fashionable, trendy.

22. Table of Characteristics

Accuracy: Careful placing of *i*-dots, exact *t*-bar crossing, legible writing and medium-sized, fast script.

Aggression: Angular strokes, triangles in lower zone *g*s and *y*s, *t*-bar.

Ambition: Rising baseline, upward slope of writing, large capitals in signature, firm downstrokes.

Brutality: Thick writing, pasty script, blunt ending of small *e*, slow pace and smeary look, sharpened *t*-bars.

Caution: Upright script, *i*-dot to left of stem, careful formation of individual letters, slow speed.

Compulsiveness: Too much uniformity of letters, narrow strokes, connected script.

Conceit: Large capitals, exaggerated size of signature, embellishments of letters.

Concentration: Small writing, neat and tidy lines, good spacing, no loops in lower zone.

Conscientiousness: Straight baseline, balanced spacing, small even letters, no left tendencies.

Creativity: Wide line spacing, slightly disconnected writing, original formations.

Cunning: Thread-like strokes tapering off into a line.

Dependability: Firm baseline, legible script, upright or right-slanted writing, *a*s and *o*s closed.

Depression: Downward-sloping lines, low *t*-bar.

Dishonesty: Varying size of letters, small *o*s open at base, left slant, pasty look.

Energy: Long loops, some angles, good pressure, *t*-bar to right.

Extravagance: Very wide left margin, exaggerated spaces between words.

Friendliness: Right slant, rounded letters, harmonious rhythm.

Humour: *T*-bar with rounded stroke, capital *I* curved.

Hysteria: Extreme 'thread' writing, dwindling strokes.

Impatience: Right slant, speedy writing, no starting strokes.

Indecision: Erratic slant left/right, uncertain pressure.

Inertia: Slow script, rounded, copybook formation, no *i*-dots, poor rhythm, weak pressure.

Inferiority complex: Small capitals, tiny *I*, small writing.

Inner conflict: Fluctuating slant, size and pressure.

Intelligence: Small writing, legible, medium capitals, quick writing, simplified style.

Jealousy: Small circle on beginning of letters.

Judgement: Lower zones without loops, right slant, well-spaced lines.

Literary ability: Greek *e* and *d*.

Materialism: Heavy pressure, full, rounded lower zones, thick *i*-dots.

Moodiness: Wavering baseline, letters bobbing up and down, changeable slant.

Nervousness: Weak pressure, light *t*-bar, short lower zones.

Objectiveness: Upright or right slant, no stroke at beginning, letters simplified.

Optimism: Rising lines.

Originality: Formations that develop away from the copybook.

Perfectionism: Tall capitals, narrow script, lean upper loops.

Perseverance: Strong *t*-bar crossing, upright writing, firm strokes, connected letters.

Pretentiousness: Looped capitals, huge *I* whirls and loops.

Reserve: Wide left margin, all-round spacing.

Rigidity: Angular strokes, rigid formations of *m* and *n*, angles.

Sarcasm: Sharpened t-bar, thin strokes, tall upper loops.

Scientific mind: Simplified forms, dots connected to next letter.

Secretiveness: Closed small *a* and *o*, enrolled *s* and some 'thread' writing.

Self-assurance: Signature larger than script, underlined and well formed, or fast script.

Sensuality: Thick pressure on downstrokes, right slant, broad letters.

Sexuality: Good pressure on downstrokes, large loops and firm strokes on *g* and *y*.

Sincerity: 'Garland' writing, increasing size of letters, and wide writing.

Spiritual interests: High upper loops, narrow and thin, accurate *t*-bar.

Sociability: Right slant, round letters and 'garland' writing.

Spontaneity: No starting strokes, fluent speed, medium-sized writing.

Stubbornness: Thick *t*-bar crossing, rigid writing.

Talkativeness: Very broad writing.

Temper: Sharpening *t*-bar crossing, thick strokes, angular *g* and *y*.

Tension: Poor flexibility between letters and words, narrow script, heavy pressure that fluctuates.

Thrift: Narrow letters, tall capitals, small *s* made like a claw.

Tidiness: Clean script, neat writing, good spacing.

Timidity: Weak *t*-bars, poor pressure, small script, under-developed lower zone, small cramped signature.

Touchiness: The same as jealousy, with loops going to right.

Toughness: Knotted small *o*s.

Unselfishness: Right slant, regular height of letters, small middle zone, extended stroke at end of small *e*.

Vitality: Normal or strong pressure, fluid script, large letters.

23. Examples of Handwriting

Male, 50s – executive

Although an executive, he is highly inhibited and has a fear of making mistakes: the wide spacing reveals his weakness. The thin, narrow angular stroke indicates his hard, ruthless nature and lack of real emotion.

A sharp, ambitious and highly neurotic personality is revealed in the abnormal squeezing together of letters.

Male, 50s – executive

Male, 55 – director

His heavy pressure and many crossings out reveal the writer to be under extreme tension and, although a speedy and clever organiser and administrator, the fluctuating slant reveals some inconsistency of character. The pressure shows that he is undermining his health and living at too high a rate of stress. This handwriting was analysed in some depth and the writer told that he should ease up on the work front, or he might be heading for a heart attack. He had a stroke one month later and died a year after.

Male, 40s – sales/marketing manager

This script with its angular strokes and left slant indicates an aggressive, introverted personality and suggests a very dominant but unco-operative man. He possesses the push and drive necessary for a high-powered job, but his relationships with subordinates are liable to be fraught owing to his aggression and sarcasm. The triangular loops to his small g and y reveal emotional and/or sexual problems, causing frustration and resentment.

Female advertising executive

Thread-like strokes reveal in the writer the ability to manipulate and a psychological talent for handling people. The fast writing shows mental agility and intelligence, but the writer may miss out on detail due to impatience. The slightly erratic size of the small letters is a sign of dislike of routine and the spacing, which is a little too wide, shows reserve in her private life. She is a good organiser but has a low boredom threshold.

Comment
The writer has a flair for intuitive thinking, is creative, persuasive and can communicate well. She displays a lack of tolerance under pressure. She may make hasty decisions, but is usually right.

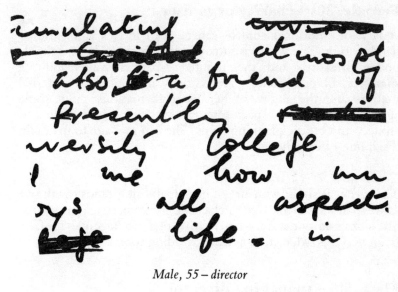

Male, 55 – director

Male, 40s – sales/marketing director

Female advertising executive

Female, 30s – charity organiser

A lack of emotional control can be seen in this right-slanted handwriting. The writer is impatient and inclined to be irritable under pressure, and the pointed *t*-bar crossings indicate sharpness of personality. She is easily influenced by external matters and the angles of her letter formations show some aggression. The poor spacing reveals weak emotions leading to anxiety and erratic planning skills. She can manage to maintain discipline – but only just.

Comment
The writer is slightly unsure of her capabilities, tends to take on more than she can manage and has a desire for prestige and status. She lacks humour and has a very low tolerance level. She suffers from nervous exhaustion at times, leading to irritability.

Male, 50s – managing director

This confident, well-spaced and formed writing (with both angles and round strokes in its letter formations) shows a dominant personality and firm character. The writer is able to take responsibility, but is also very human and generates a certain amount of warmth towards his fellows. The small closed *a*s and *o*s indicate his discretion and the large middle zone shows his need for a secure and harmonious emotional life. The long downstrokes without loops are a sign of good judgement and a healthy ego, and the right slant means that he has excellent mind control and is not going to lose his head in a crisis.

Comment
This writer displays excellent planning ability, can mix and socialise with ease at most levels and is honest and direct. He is fully aware of his own capabilities and is able to delegate and inspire others with confidence.

The people that fall into the category of
special require an adjustment of design
to suit their particular needs. These are
people who are disabled and prefer to
look after themselves.

Female, 30s – charity organiser

Would you please
three for me as
you can. They
Very important to

All are male ...

Male, 50s – managing director

Bibliography

Green, James, and Lewis, David, *The Hidden Language of Your Handwriting*, 1980. Souvenir Press.

Hartford, Huntington, *You Are What You Write: Handwriting Analysis*, 1975. Peter Owen.

Jung, Carl, *Four Archetypes: Mother, Rebirth, Spirit, Trickster*, 1986. Ark Publications.

Hearns, Rudolph S. *Handwriting Analysis Through its Symbolism*, 2nd edn, 1979. The American Association of Handwriting Analysts.

Jung, Carl. *Man and His Symbols*, 1983. Picador.

Marcuse, Irene, *A Guide to the Disturbed Personality*, 1969. Arco Publishing, New York.

Mendel, Alfred, *Personality in Handwriting*, 1947. Stephen Daye Press, New York.

Olyanova, Nadya, *Handwriting Tells*, 1969. Wilshire, USA.

Olyanova, Nadya, *The Psychology of Handwriting*, 1960. Wilshire, USA.

Saudek, Robert. *The Psychology of Handwriting*, 1978. Books for Professionals.

Singer, Eric. *A Manual of Graphology*, 3rd edn, 1987. Duckworth.

Roman, Klara G. *Handwriting, A Key to Personality*, 1952. Pantheon.